Jack Pierson
New Pieces

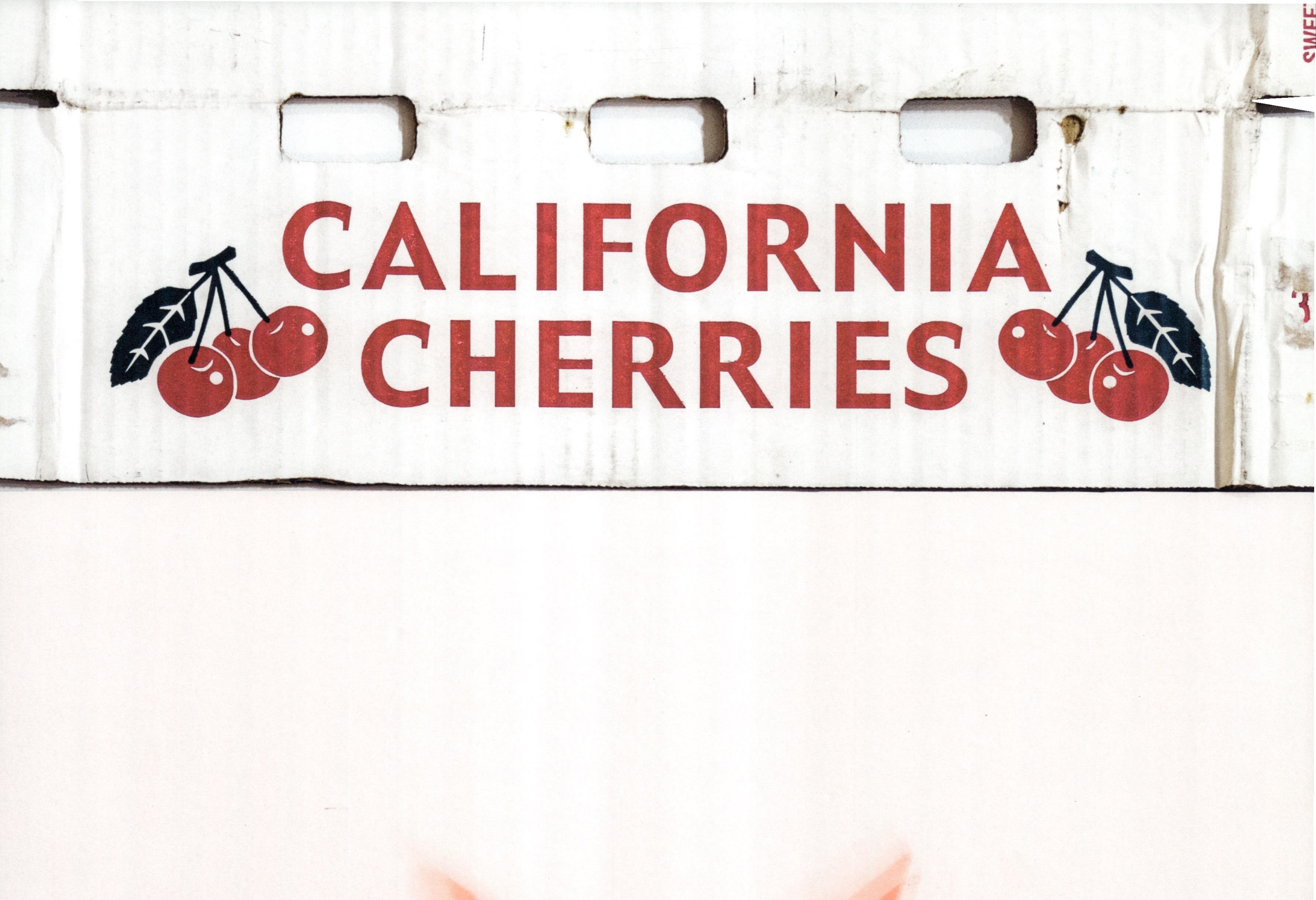

CALIFORNIA
CHERRIES
SWEET

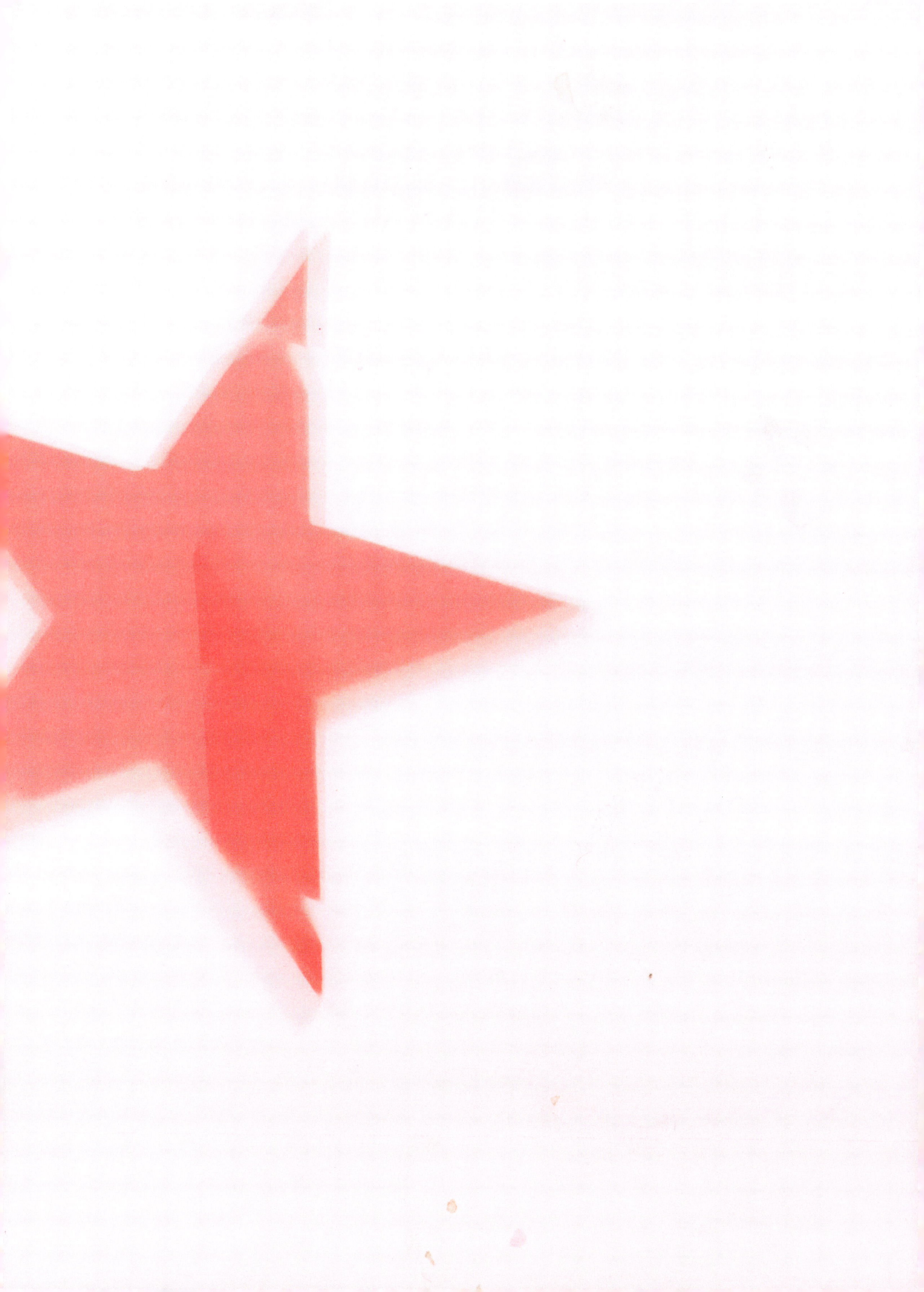

Consider the Magpie
Bonnie Morrison

2020 surely meant different things to everyone, but it would seem easy
make the case that the thing that every single one of us did was spend quite
a bit of time in contemplation of the spaces we inhabit, of surroundings
large and small.

Who else occupied this world around us?

What of our world had we never before really seen?

What is time when no one need rush?

Endless.

Or space, when plazas are stripped of crowd and clutter?

Vast, as it turns out.

Even in places like New York City.

And that notes may still — or newly — be heard when the noisiest beats
are gone?

This one can be answered quite literally: it's Birdsong.

When the traffic stopped and the kitchens closed, gates were padlocked
and generators switched off, the early weeks and months of the Pandemic
revealed that on any given day, each and every city and town is full of calling,
chattering, riotously chirping birds. And not just pigeons! Our skies are
filled with sparrows, starlings, warblers, finches.

Nightjars, curassows, and finfoots.

Grebes, guans, cuckoos.

Francolins, chacalacas, potoos.

Magpies.

Like its cousin the crow, the Magpie is no mere contender for valedictorian
of the Class *Aves*. It's more of a National Merit Scholar, sharing the stage with

elephants, whales and orangutans. Able to solve puzzles, as well as recognize its own face in a mirror. Big-brained, but with vitality and spark as well: the Magpie of lore is a matchmaker with legendary taste, drawn to shiny, eye-catching things that it selects, then stashes. Might be chunk of this, or a chip of that; it knows what it likes.

It's why people given to amassing alluring objects — those types who can't help but brake for a ribbon, remnant, marble, medal, flyer, wrapper or charm — describe themselves this way, a whole species as defining characteristic: "*I'm a such a magpie.*" They identify deeply with this avian curator of the souvenirs of all its departures and landings. It seems quite natural, we think, that a creature possessed of such estimable intelligence and memory is a born collector.

Us too.

So it is this clever bird's tune that the viewer may imagine presiding over the days that hatched these new pieces. Yes, these massive collages invoke the beloved, oft-imitated word installations of their maker, but formally speak-ing, they are quite far from work whose signature is letter-perfection. This is wholly new vocabulary, formulated from the genuine ephemera of Pierson's existence. The messages here have shrugged off their Before-Times syntax to form a constitution whose very constitution is the story of how a Life of Creation translates Life on Pause. How might an artist best known for commu-nicating via devices (words, cameras) that suppose an audience (or at least a subject) adapt to the sudden, radical remove of both? What would he be left to work with?

Objects found in the nest, of course.

Some of these items are immediately familiar and, we might guess, had been diligently preserved until their conscription. But what is also abundantly clear is that each grouping contains elements that never dared hope to tread a path to any collector's wall. These are things that Pierson has accumulated as well as the things that have no doubt accumulated *around* him. To be fabricated in the year everything took on different meaning is also to take every fabricated thing's meaning different(ly).

And the dimension of these assemblages! Pierson's sly gift to us after so many months of squinting at various brands of tiny squares and rectangles. The overhead 2D of *Pink* is both snapshot and enlargement, diagramming that "approved in-person gathering" – the picnic. The mirror-like surface and architectural soar of *Empire* conveys what those accustomed to flight know intimately: the skyline viewed fully and at great height is the version most familiar of all. And *Xerox*'s three yards of black plastic suggests the coast of Atlantic City in the minutes before Johnnie Taylor prepares to take the stage on a Summer night. Life at a distance: new, perhaps, to us, but so familiar to that thing with feathers.

Did Pierson always dream of that Adidas shade of *Blue*, the sculptural qualities of the foam insulation he uses for *Ode,* or any of these odds and ends, really? Perhaps not, but their application is a poignant reminder of all we've come to know about the Beauty of Necessity — as well as the Necessity of Beauty. There are sources that say the magpie seeks the "valuable," but you might also hear its trove described this way: *things of significance*. This is the other bird's Eye: gathering, preserving. Elevating, repurposing, renewing. Rising, and flying again.

And what could feel more precious or true after months of enforced isolation? Who among us has not, during this time, gazed at a ticket stub or matchbook from a venue now closed — perhaps forevermore — with the emotion previously reserved for heirlooms, or the image of a loved one? These works reveal the double helix of that particular romance; a strain of Nostalgia previously unknown.

All art holds within it some very literal reference to time. Passing and slowing, bending and curving, darting and braking, building up and falling away. The photograph is its instant, while the canvas or statue may represent years. But these? These are the *actual* receipts. The things we used, the things we kept. Some packaging, a bag, a layer of adhesive, an expanse of cloth. More than their form or function, they are mementos that say:

I was there.

You were too.

We were together.

May we be again.

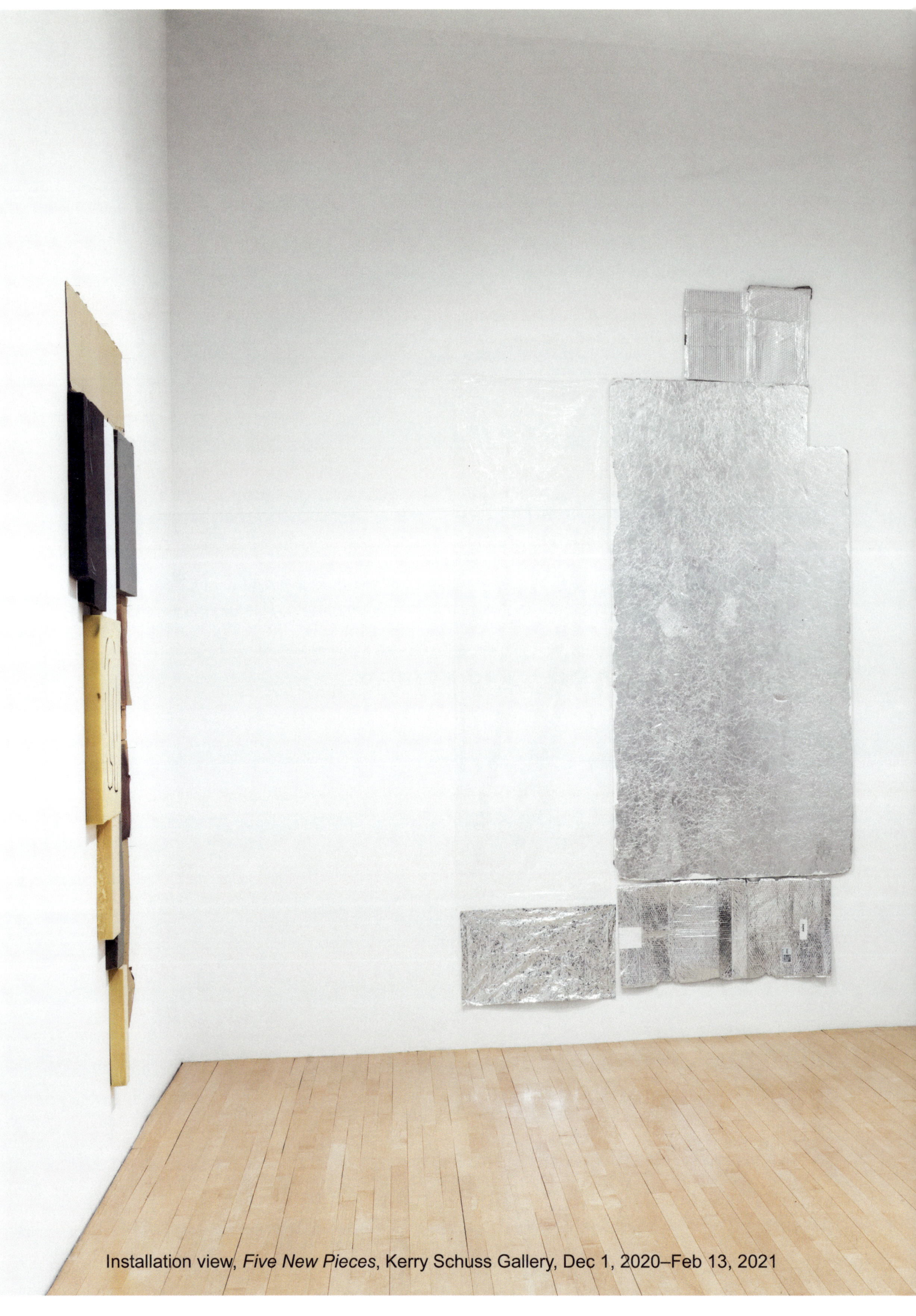

Installation view, *Five New Pieces*, Kerry Schuss Gallery, Dec 1, 2020–Feb 13, 2021

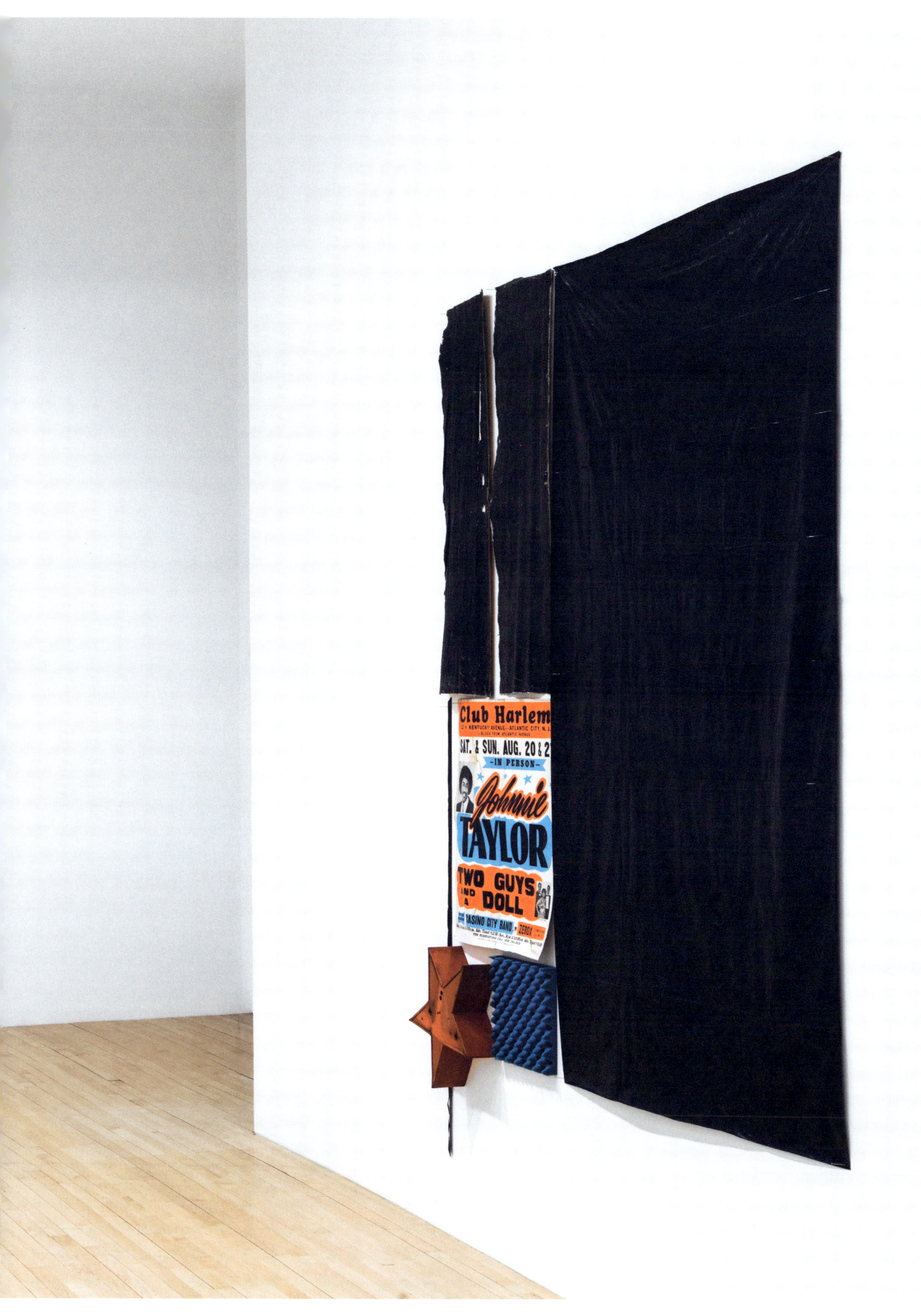

Club Harlem
32 N. KENTUCKY AVENUE -- ATLANTIC CITY, N. J.
½ BLOCK FROM ATLANTIC AVENUE
SAT. & SUN. AUG. 20 & 2
-IN PERSON-
Johnnie
TAYLOR
TWO GUYS
AND A DOLL
CASINO CITY BAND + ZEROX
FOR RESERVATIONS CALL

First One, 2020
Bankers pins, cardboard, and paper
85⅝ × 82½ × 2 inches

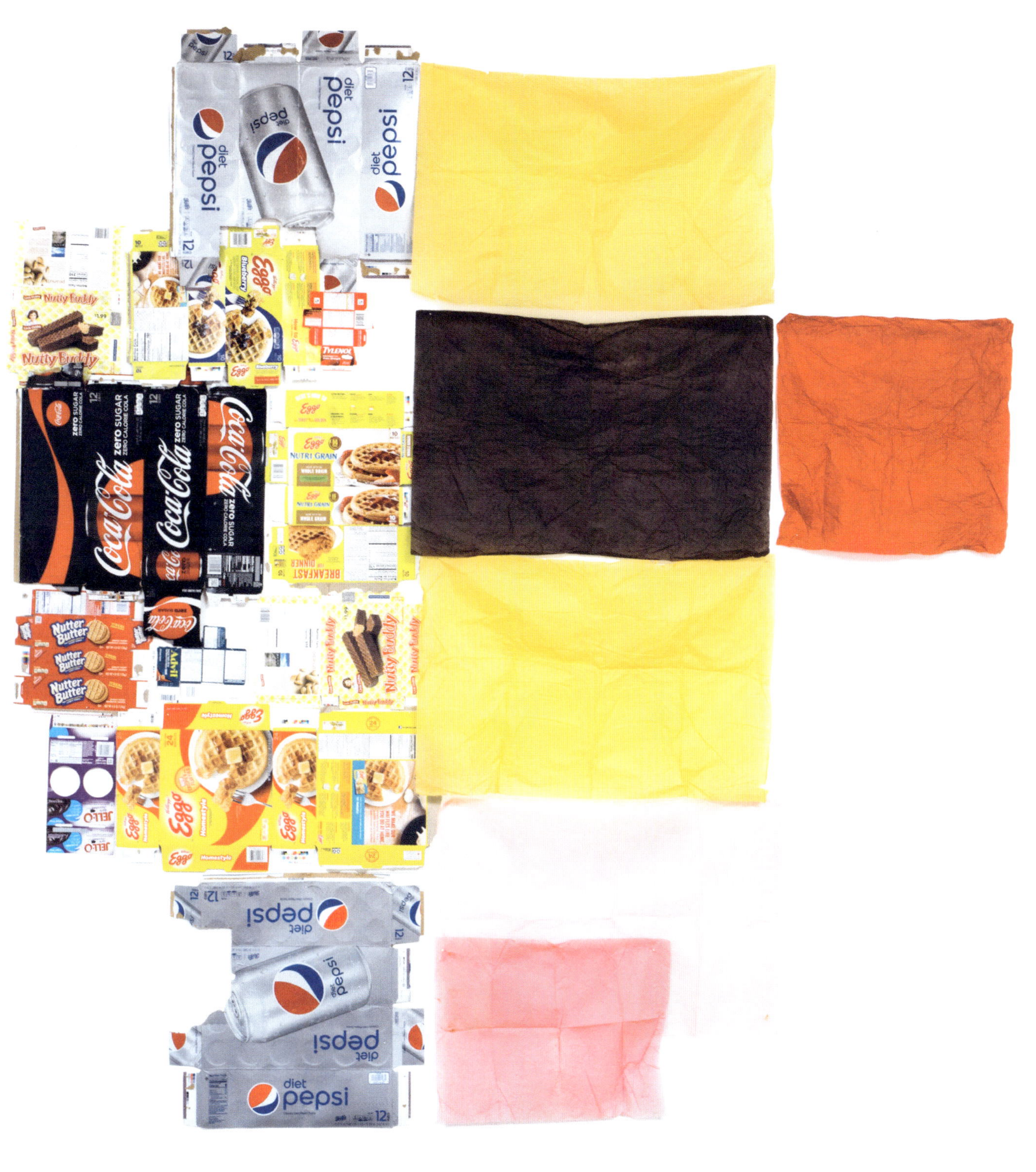

Ginger Ganesha, 2020
Bankers pins, cardboard, cloth,
and paper
92 × 59½ × 2 inches

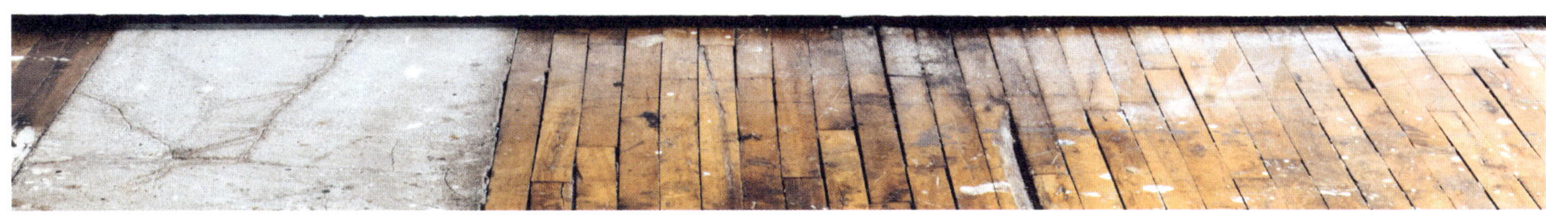

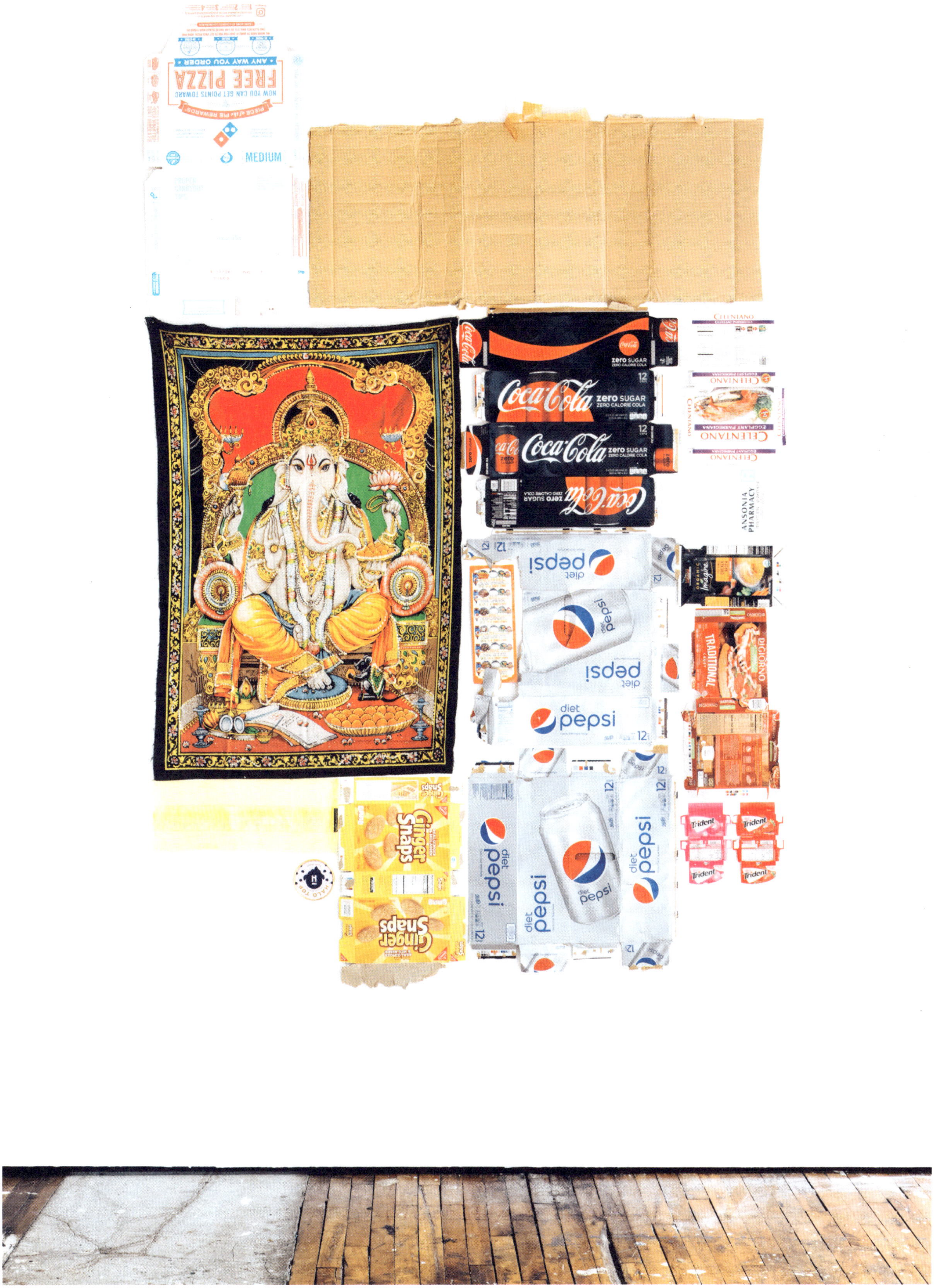

Yellow, 2020
Bankers pins, cardboard, and paper
67 × 56 × 2 inches

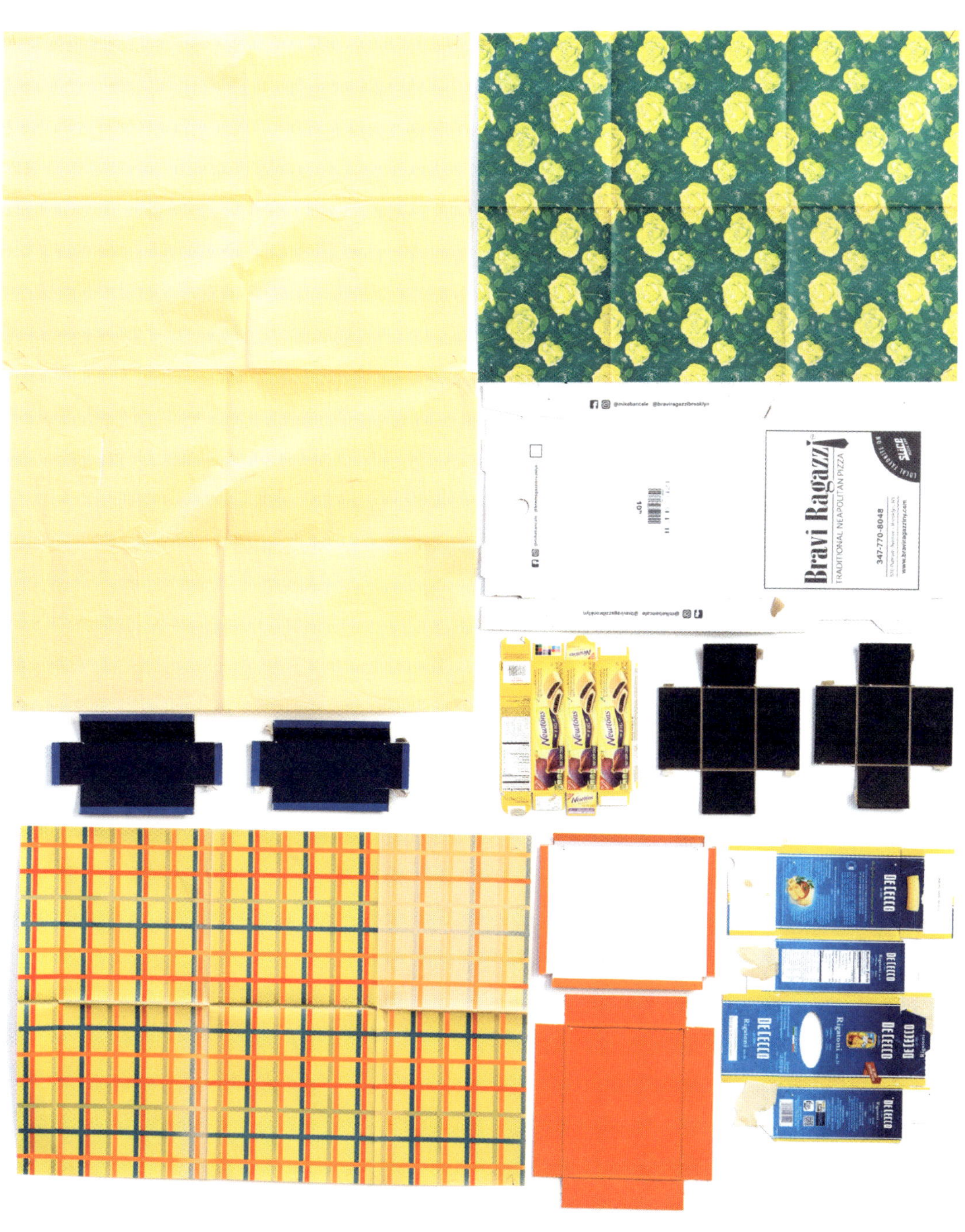

Blue, 2020
Bankers pins, cardboard, paper,
and spray paint
110 × 65 × 4 inches

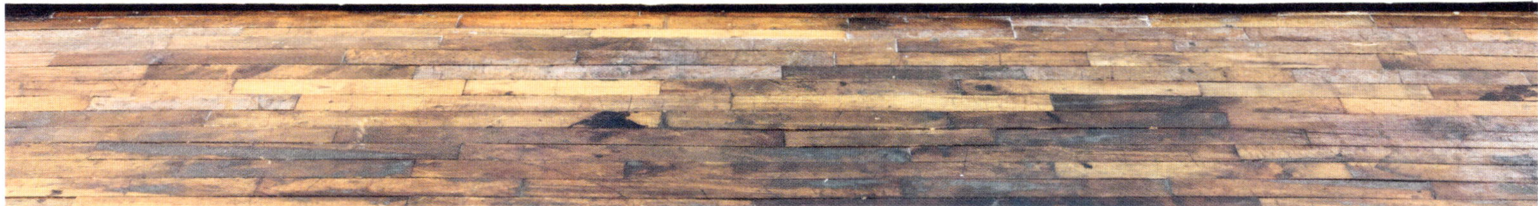

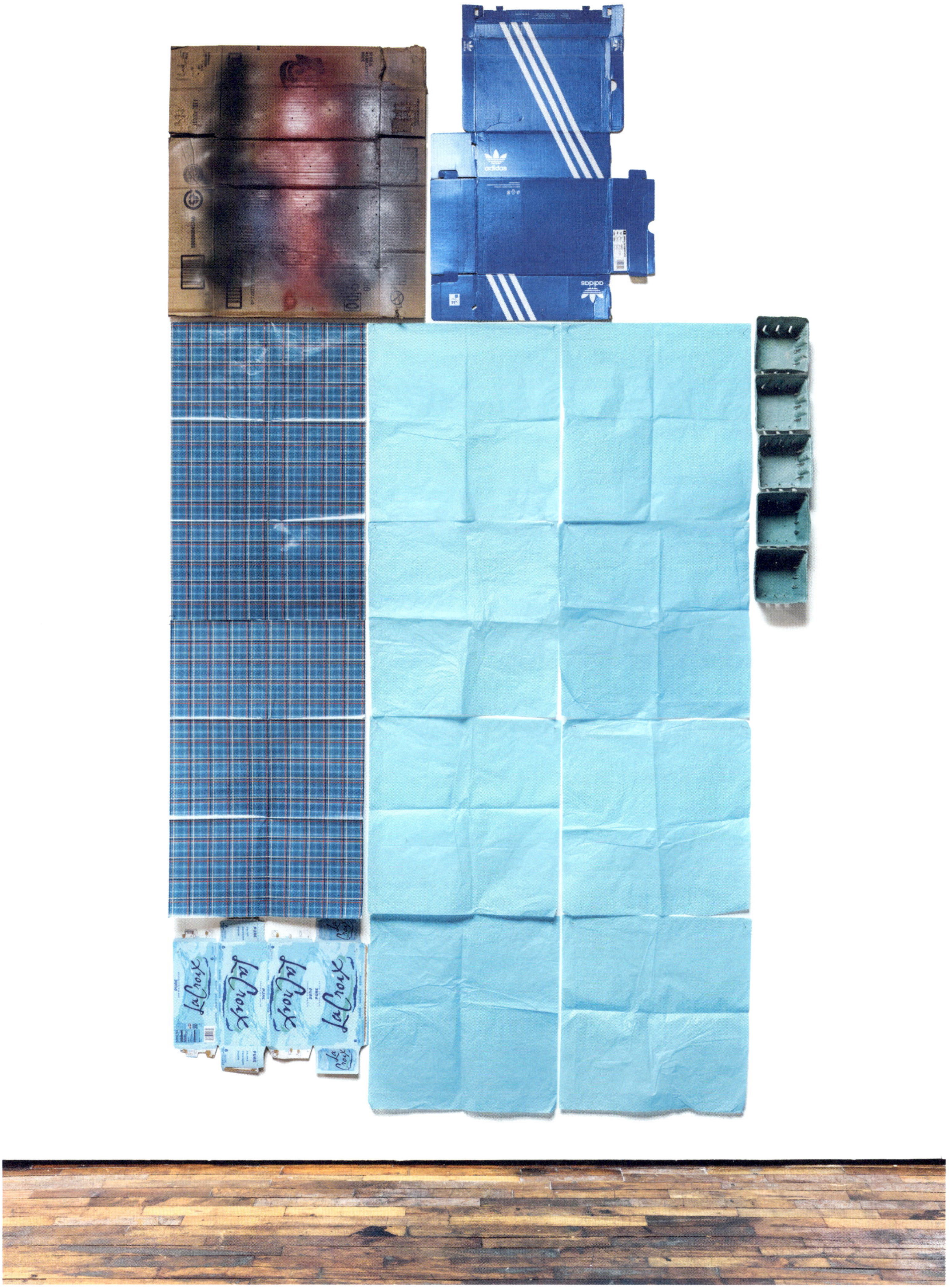

Pink, 2020
Bankers pins, cardboard, cloth,
and foamcore
89 × 85 × 2 inches

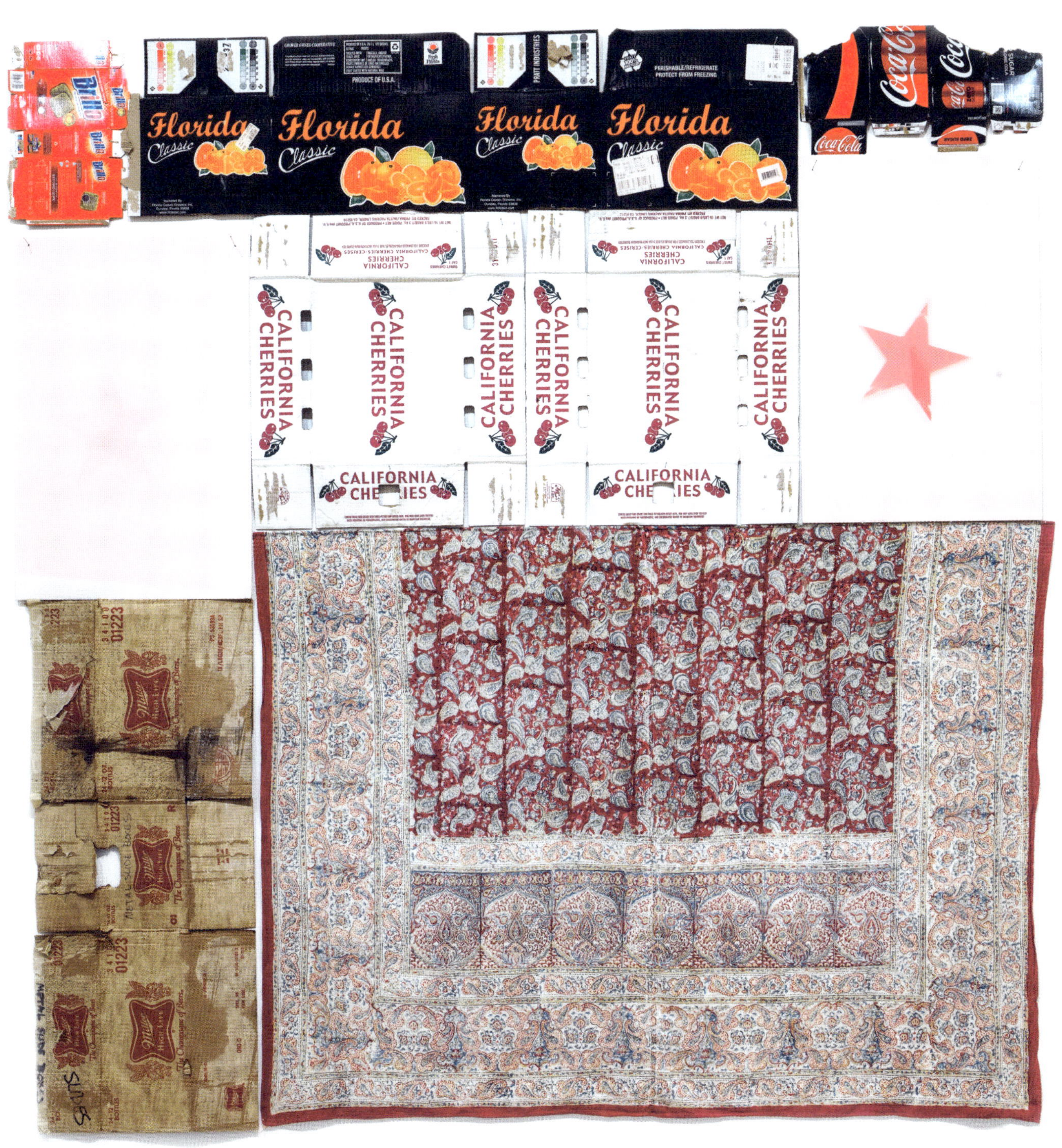

Xerox, 2020
Bankers pins, cardboard, foam
rubber, metal, plastic, and ribbon
102 × 73 × 4½ inches

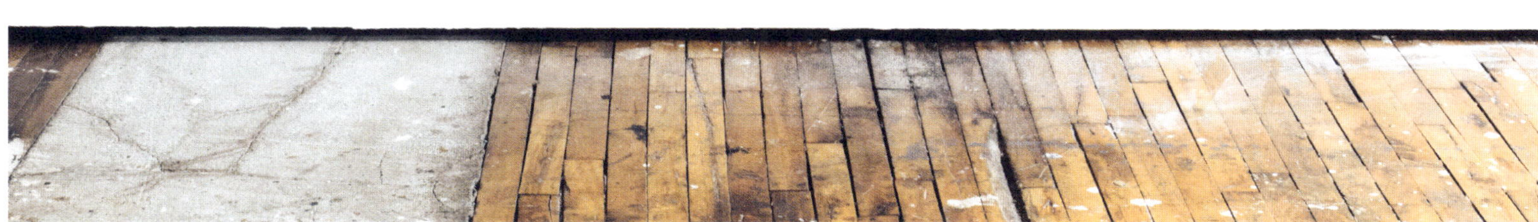

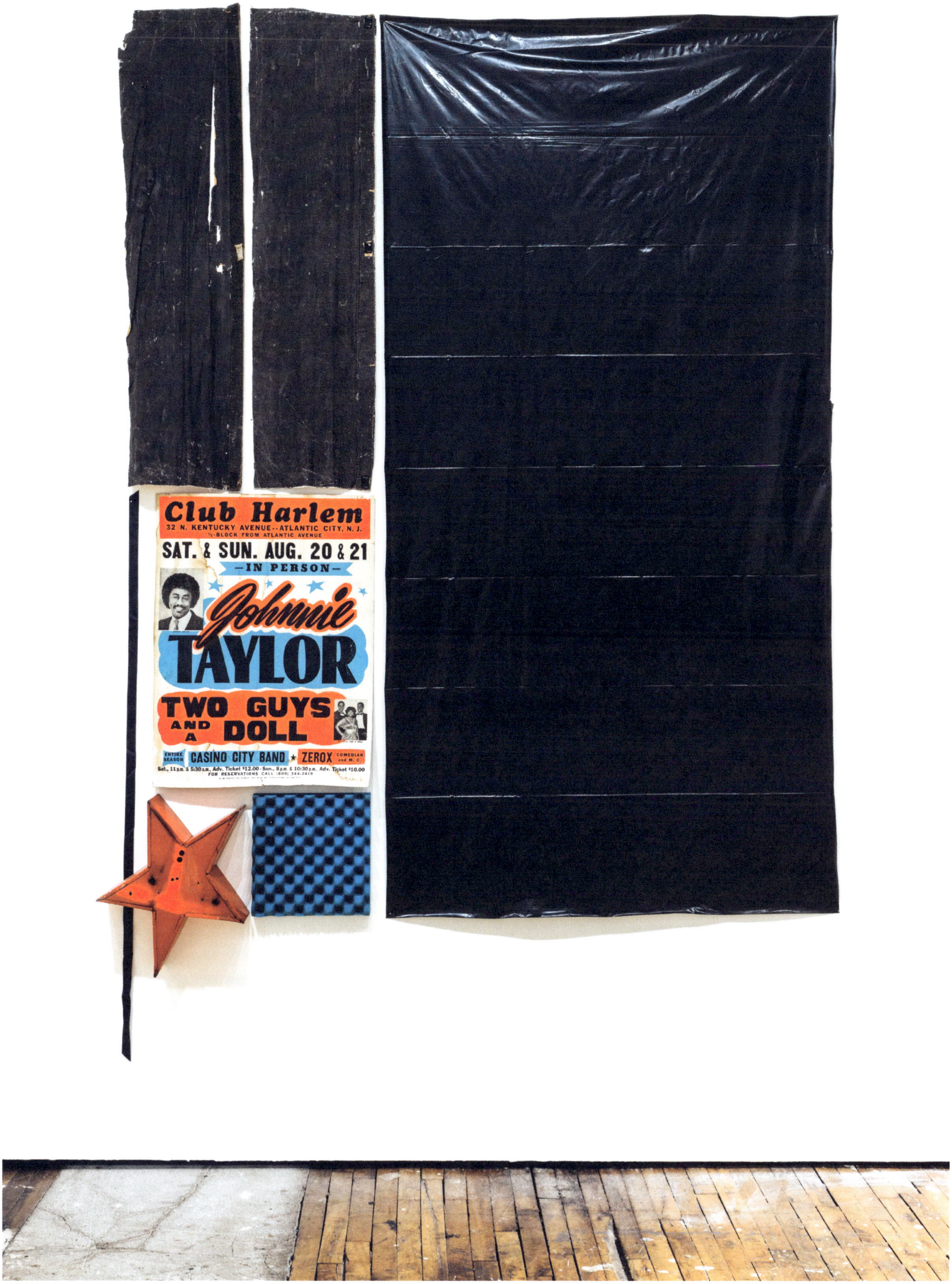

Club Harlem
32 N. KENTUCKY AVENUE--ATLANTIC CITY, N.J.
½-BLOCK FROM ATLANTIC AVENUE
SAT. & SUN. AUG. 20 & 21
—IN PERSON—
Johnnie TAYLOR
TWO GUYS AND A DOLL
ENTIRE SEASON CASINO CITY BAND ★ ZEROX COMEDIAN and M.C.
Sat., 11 p.m. & 5:30 a.m. Adv. Ticket $12.00 - Sun., 8 p.m. & 10:30 p.m. Adv. Ticket $10.00
FOR RESERVATIONS CALL (609) 344-2419

Berries, 2020
Bankers pins, paper, and plastic
40 × 18½ × 4 inches

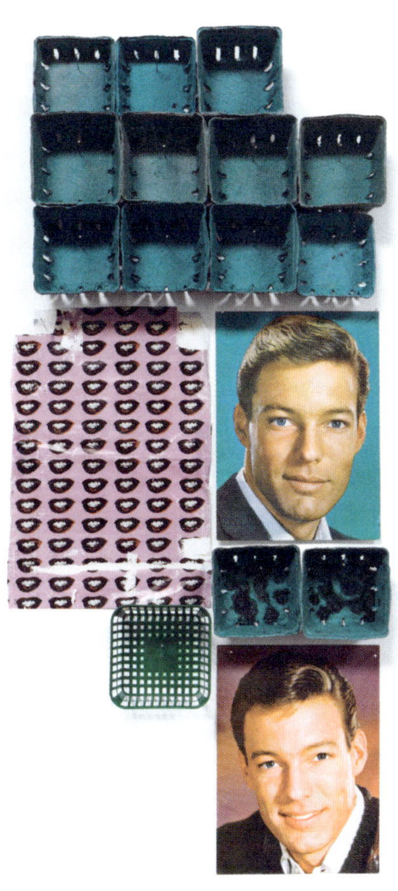
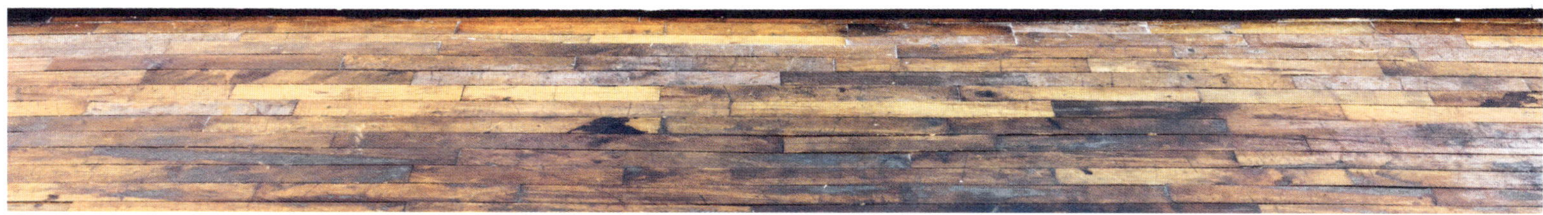

Tostito, 2020
Bankers pins, cardboard, paper,
and plastic
45½ × 78½ × 2½ inches

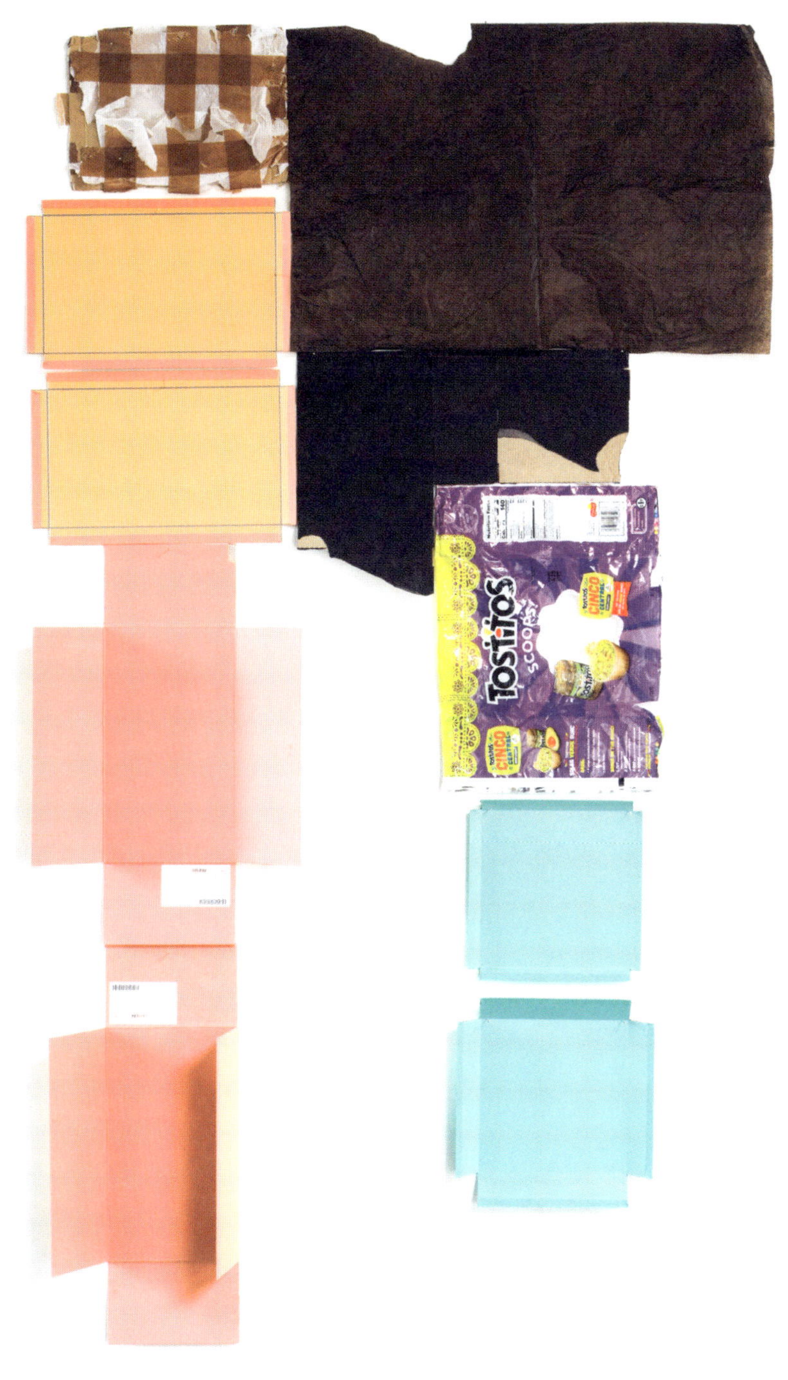
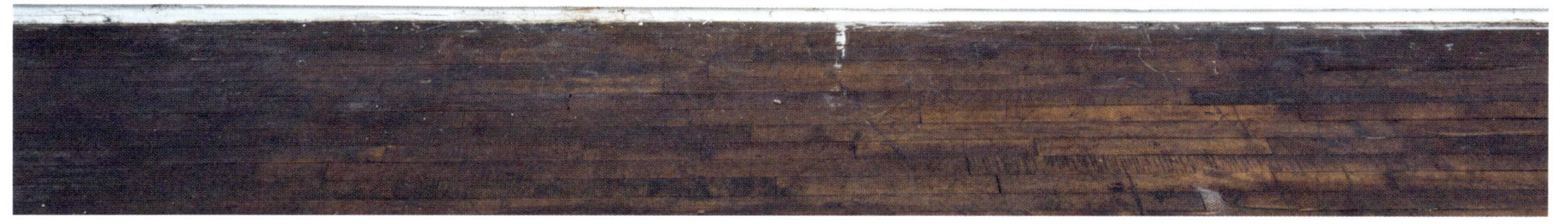

Black and Blue, 2020
Bankers pins, cardboard, newsprint,
paper, pastels, and spraypaint
54 × 21 × 2½ inches

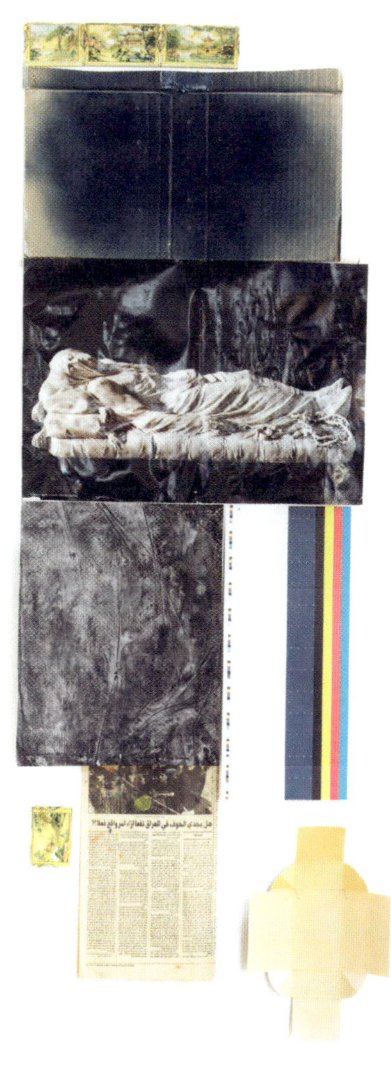

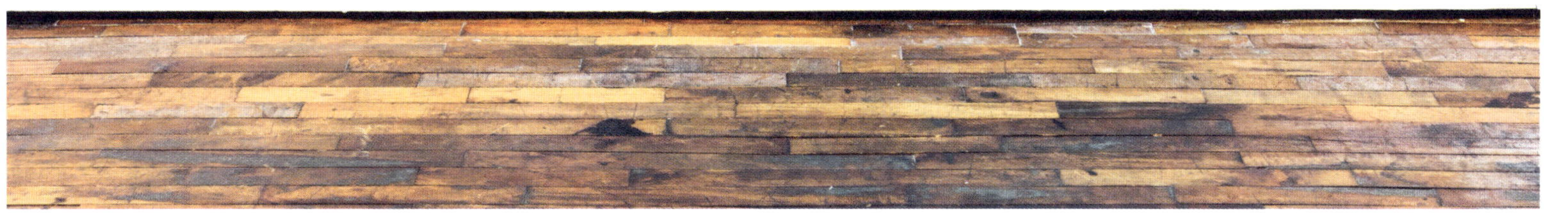

Sunrise, Goa, 2021
Bankers pins, cardboard, cloth,
foam, mylar, plastic, and sequins
99½ × 101 × 4 inches

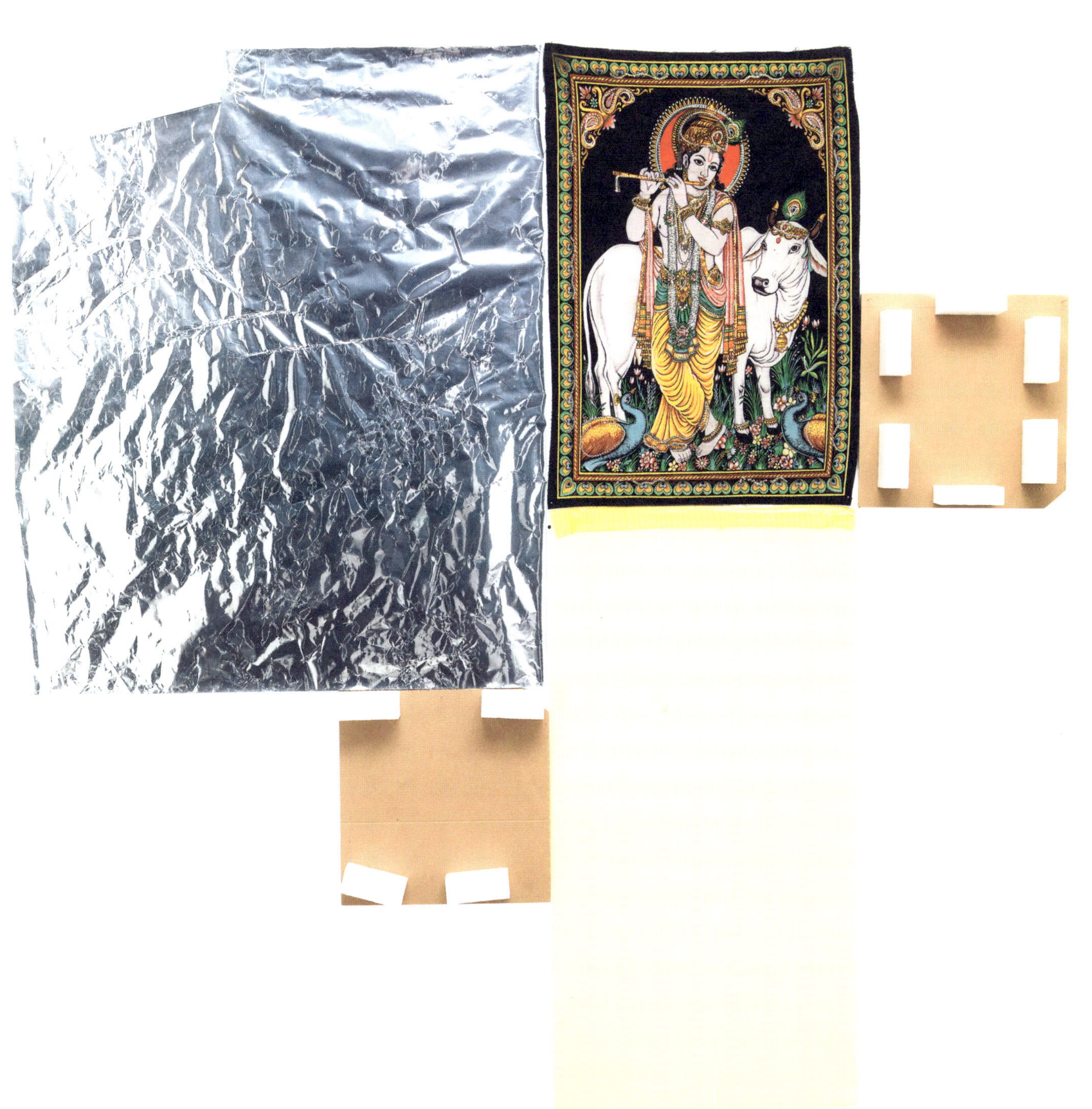

Ode, 2020
Bankers pins, cardboard, foam
rubber, spray paint, and styrofoam
98 × 52½ × 2½ inches

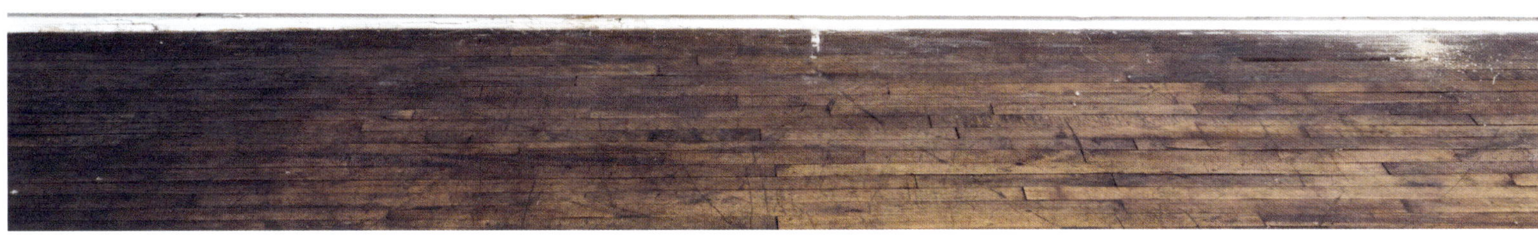

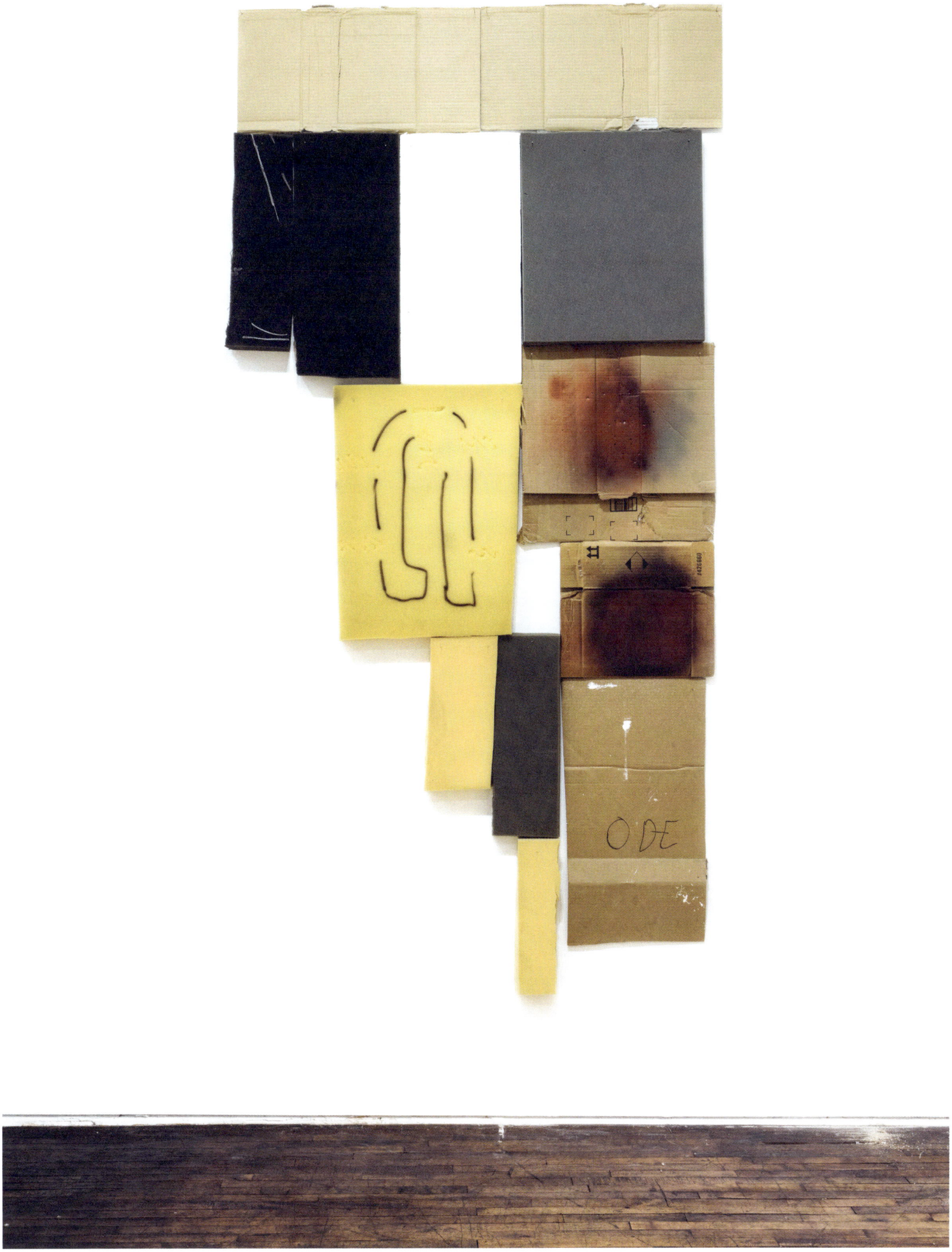

Sad, 2020
Bankers pins, cardboard,
packaging, and foam rubber
36½ × 41½ × 2½ inches

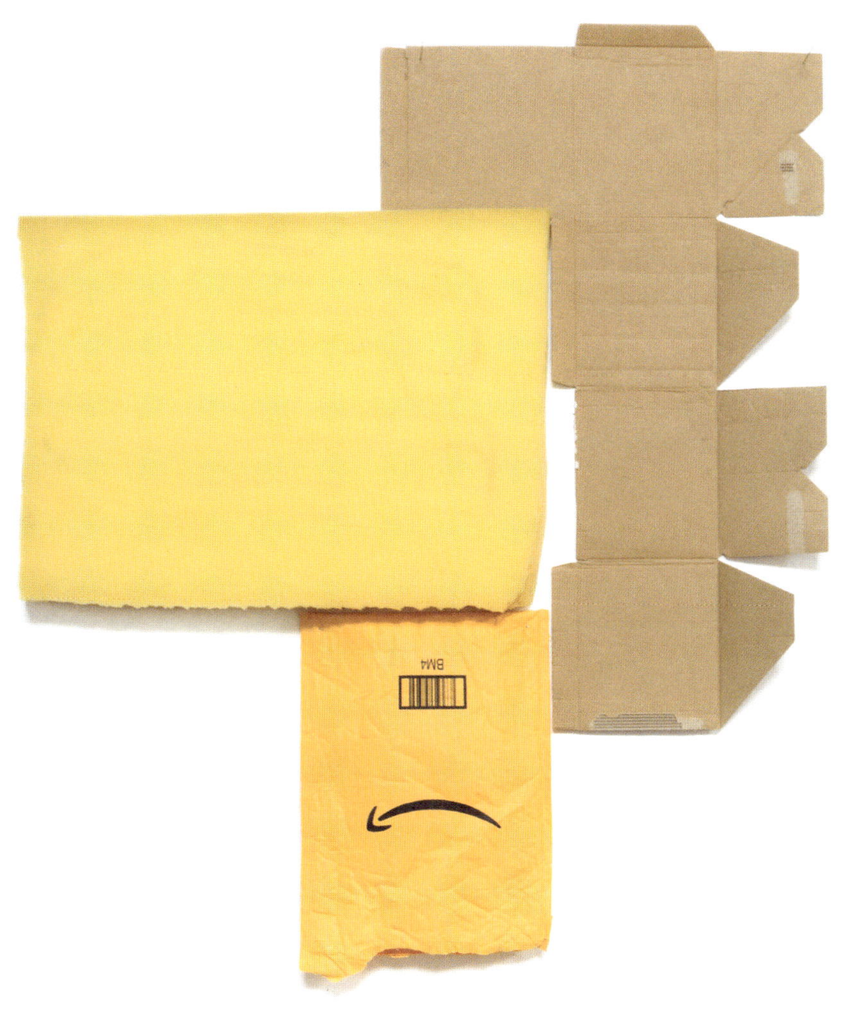

BM4

Empire, 2020
Aluminum foil, bankers pins,
envelopes, foamcore, and plastic
137 × 77½ × 2 inches

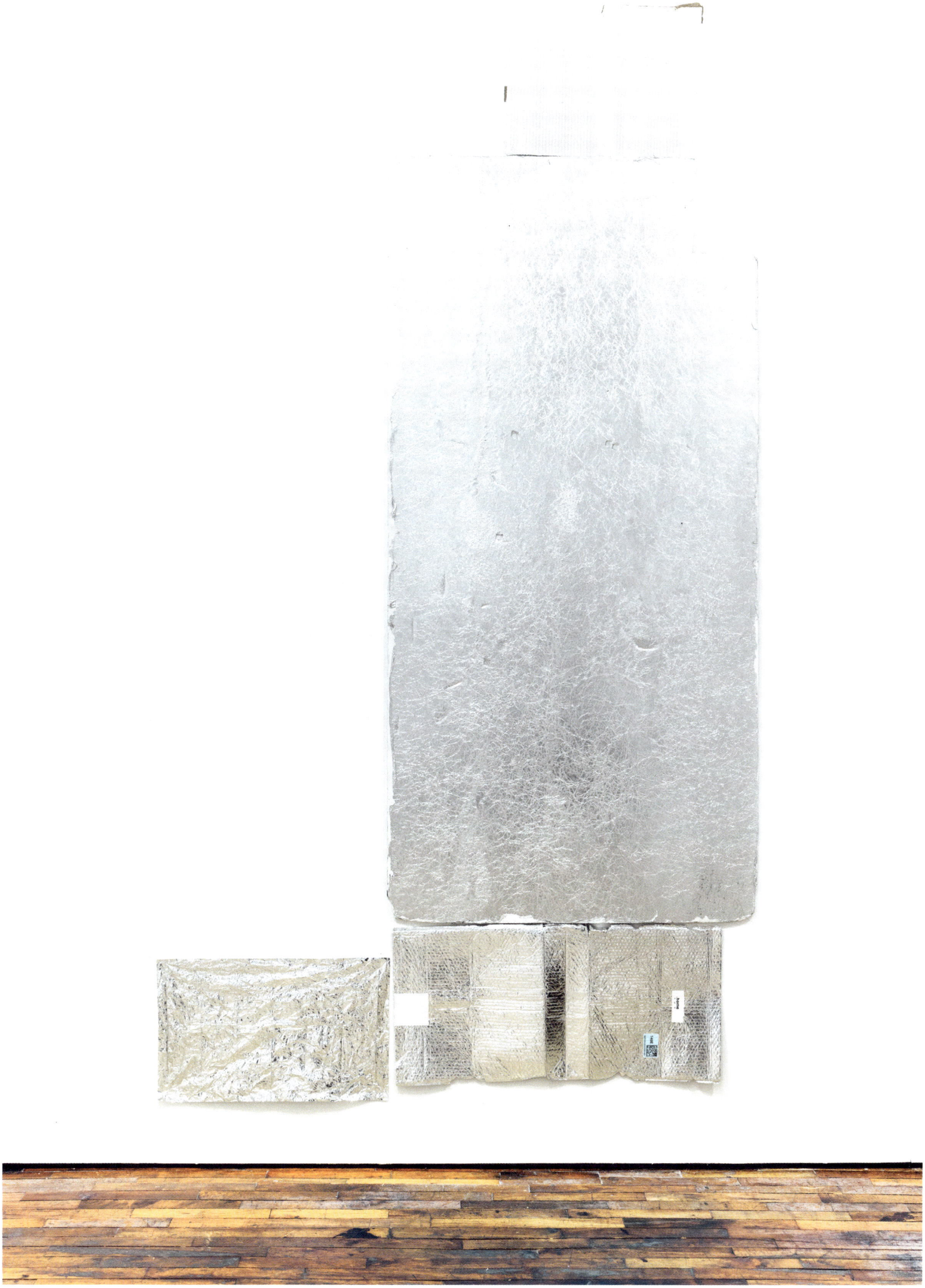

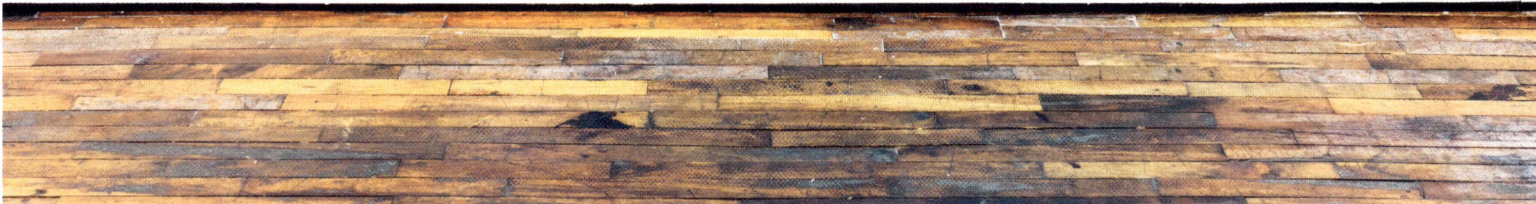

Tribute, 2020
Bankers pins, foam rubber,
and styrofoam
66½ × 88 × 2½ inches

Cloud, 2021
Bankers pins, plastic, and styrofoam
100 × 39¼ × 2½ inches

Truro Too, 2021
Archival pigment print, bankers pins,
and foam rubber
88 × 69 × 2½ inches

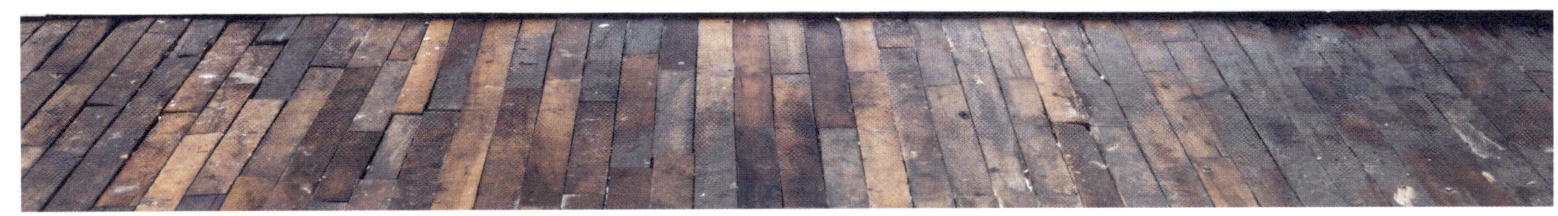

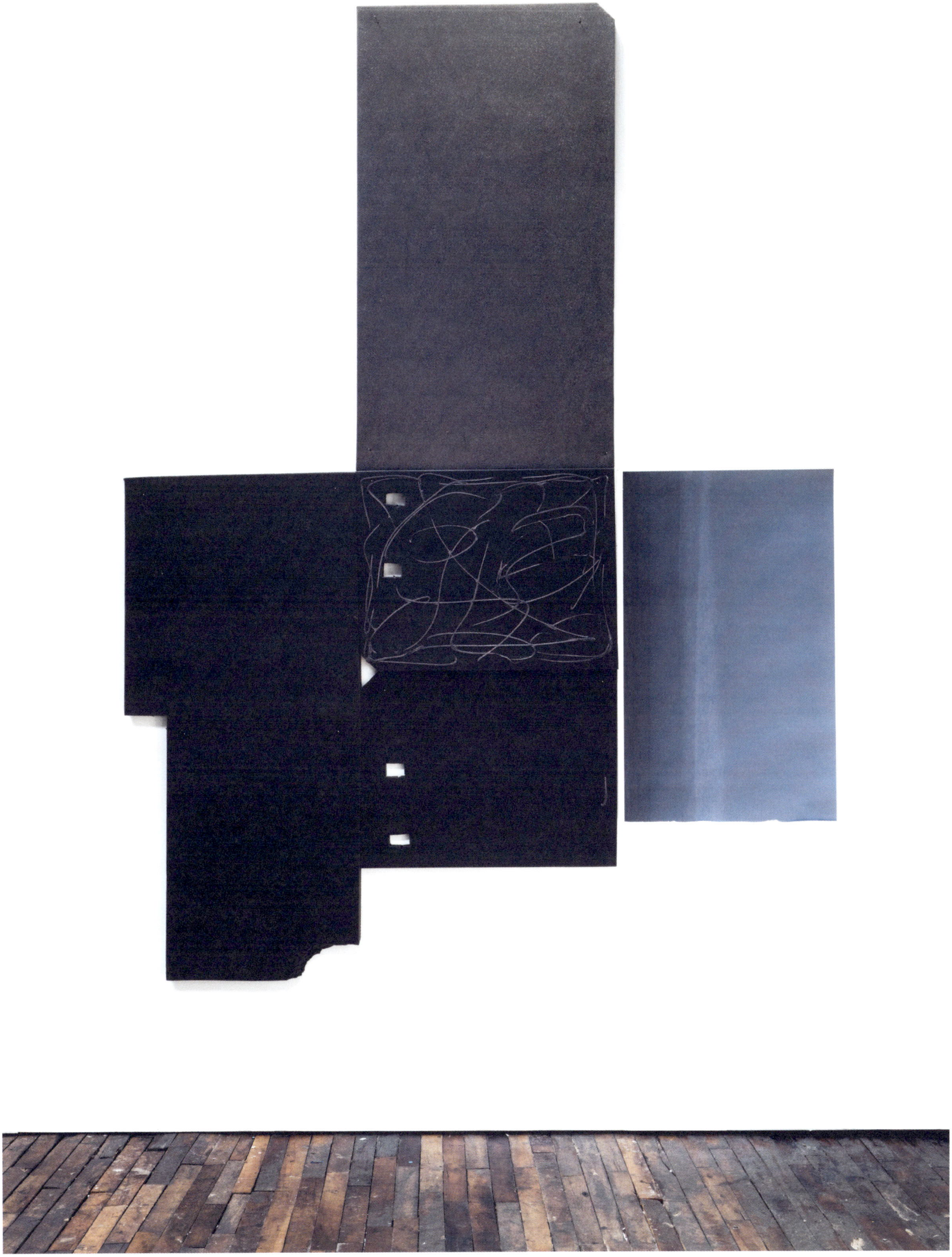

Mint Secession, 2021
Bankers pins, bubble wrap,
gaffer tape, and masking tape
64 × 50½ × ½ inches

2 Weeks in the Desert, 2021
Bankers pins and wrapping paper
90 × 78½ × ½ inches

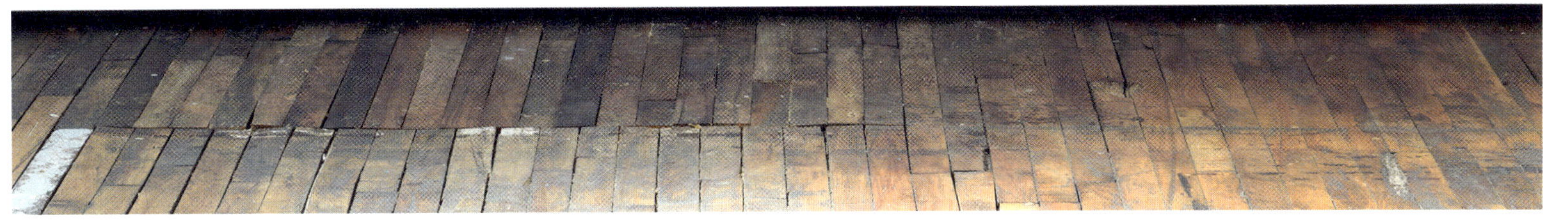

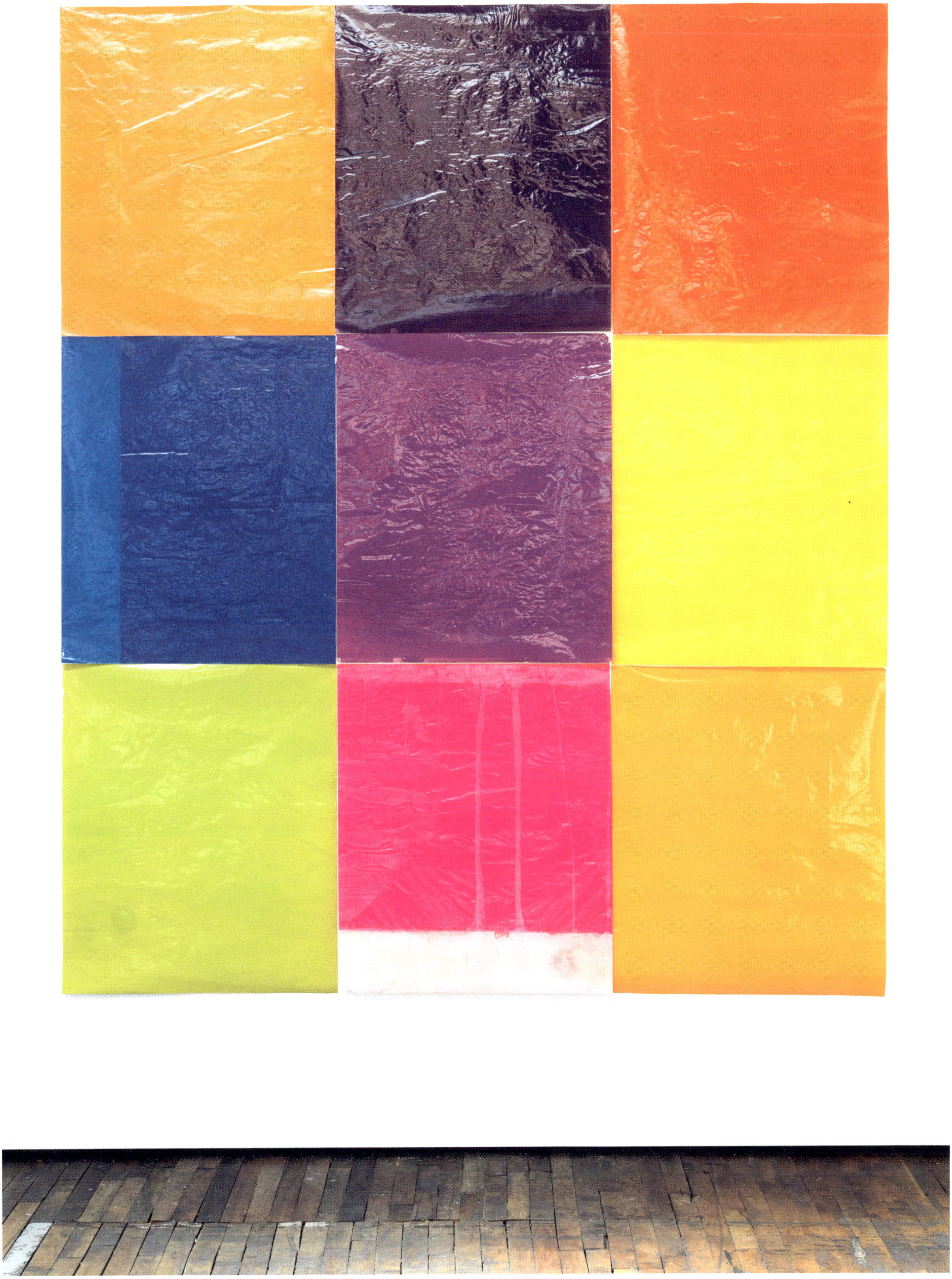

SPARKLING WATER
PURE
0-CALORIE
0-SWEETENER
0-SODIUM
=INNOCENT!
8 SPARKLING CANS
355 mL (2.84 L)
12 FL OZ (96 FL OZ)

LaCroix
PURE
SPARKLING WATER

0-CALORIE 0-SWEETENER 0-SODIUM = INNOCENT!

Nutrition Facts
8 servings per container
Serving size 1 Can
Amount per serving
Calories 0
% Daily Value
Total Fat 0g 0%
Sodium 0mg 0%
Total Carbohydrate 0g 0%
Protein 0g
Not a significant source of saturated fat, trans fat, cholesterol, dietary fiber, total sugars, added sugars, vitamin D, calcium, iron, and potassium.

INGREDIENTS: CARBONATED WATER. NON-GMO

DISTRIBUTED BY
LACROIX BEVERAGES, INC.,
A NATIONAL BEVERAGE COMPANY.
26901 INDUSTRIAL BLVD.
HAYWARD, CA 94545
©2019 CT LIC #249
PRODUCT OF USA
100% RECYCLABLE
lacroixwater.com
1-888-241-7360

NON GMO PROJECT VERIFIED
WHOLE30 approved
PLEASE RECYCLE

0 12993 22133 1

WestRock FRIDGEMASTER

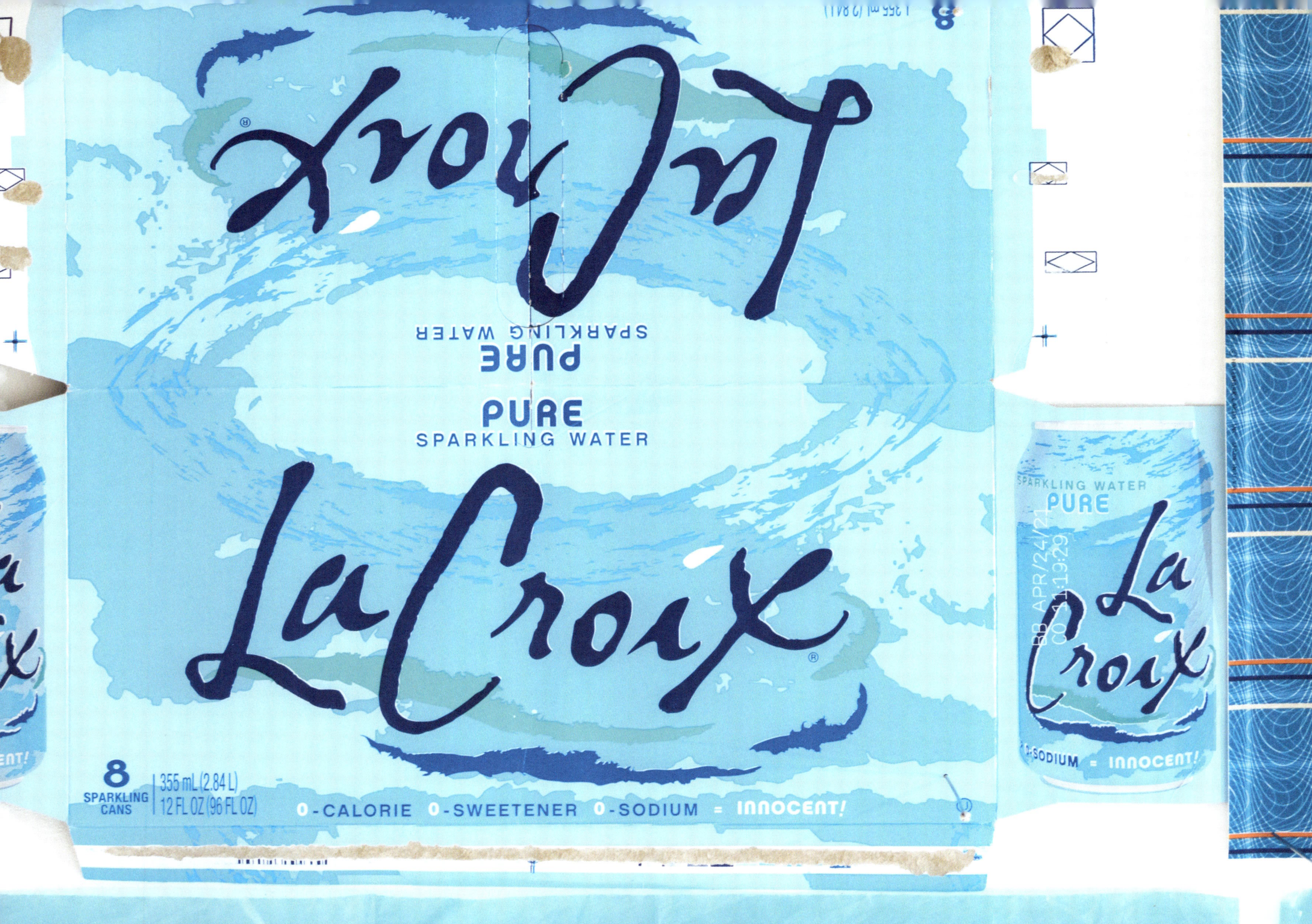

LaCroix
PURE
SPARKLING WATER
PURE
SPARKLING WATER
LaCroix
8
SPARKLING CANS
355 mL (2.84 L)
12 FL OZ (96 FL OZ)
0-CALORIE 0-SWEETENER 0-SODIUM = INNOCENT!
SPARKLING WATER
PURE
La Croix
BB APR/24/21
CO 11:19:29
SODIUM = INNOCENT!

Jack Pierson
New Pieces

Published by
Hassla Books

Edition of 500

Publication © 2021
Hassla and Jack Pierson

Artwork © Jack Pierson

Consider the Magpie © Bonnie Morrison

ISBN 978-1-940881-43-0